Carving Seasonal Decorations
For Windows & Door Frames

D1567692

Paul & Camille Bolinger

4880 Lower Valley Road, Atglen, PA 19310 USA

Contents

Copyright © 1999 by Paul & Camille Bolinger
Library of Congress Catalog Card Number:98-89439

Book Designed by Randy L. Hensley
Type set in Benguiat Bk BT/Souvenir Lt BT

ISBN: 0-7643-0715-0

Printed in China

Published by Schiffer Publishing Ltd.
4880 Lower Valley Road
Atglen, PA 19310
Phone: (610) 593-1777; Fax: (610) 593-2002
E-mail: Schifferbk@aol.com
Please visit our web site catalog at www.schifferbooks.com
or write for a free catalog.
This book may be purchased from the publisher.
Please include $3.95 for shipping.

In Europe, Schiffer books are distributed
by
Bushwood Books
6 Marksbury Rd.
Kew Gardens
Surrey TW9 4JF England
Phone: 44 (0)181 392-8585; Fax: 44
(0)181 392-9876
E-mail: Bushwd@aol.com

Please try your bookstore first.

We are interested in hearing from authors
with book ideas on related subjects.

Dedication

Once more I must praise and thank my great family. Thank you Camille for your help and inspiration. Thank you Jake for your stalwart friendship and understanding. Both of you provide the most wonderful home and family life that could possibly exist. I love you both.

Acknowledgments

For the fifth time Pat McChesney came riding in like the cavalry with his camera, lights, and talent to save our bacon. This time, in order to have a correct view, Pat had to stand on a ladder through the entire carving process, perching precariously between the lighting umbrellas and at times hanging with the camera over the bench. Never once did he complain, but more importantly he never fell onto the work either. Falling onto my carving bench loaded with sharp tools would have been just one more incident to add to Pat's year which already has included being knocked out by the family horse. Thanks again Pat.

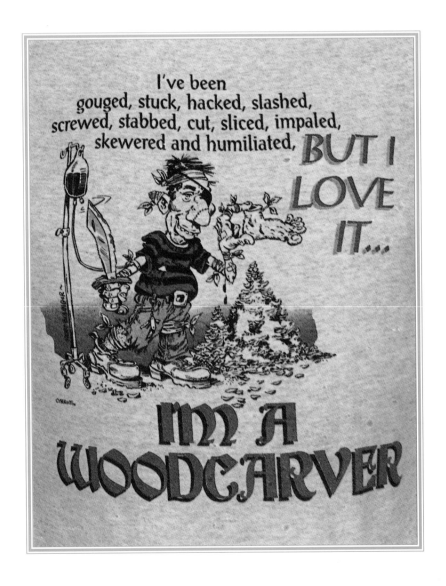

Introduction

During the building process for our home in Spokane, Washington, Camille decided she would like to upgrade the interior doors from hollow core to solid wood doors. While this would give a beautiful warm feeling to our home, there were 23 doors to be upgraded, leaving us with a lot of wood molding for potential decorative work.

Sometime during the long winter Camille and I came up with the idea of carving decorative items that could rest atop the door frame molding. From this we also thought up the idea of having a piece that would sit on top of the molding and extend to hang down one side or the other. The idea of adding a hanging element to the pieces enhanced the designs and made them much more eye-catching. Naturally, one's eye tends to follow the molding around a door. The hanging aspect of these carvings breaks up the visual flow of the sides and top molding of the door frame, making the piece jump out at you.

Most of the walls in our house are painted white which provides a great background for these designs. The bright colors in the designs show up well against the white walls and the rich golden brown color of the wood molding around the doors. The designs will work with other wall and trim colors, but you may need to modify the color scheme of the pieces depending on you specific background colors.

We designed these pieces for door tops, but they work just as well above windows, cabinets, and on some frames. I'm sure you will find the perfect spot in your home for your carvings.

Chapter One
A Corner for Every Season

Camille and I have been doing designs for the gift industry for the past five years but have concentrated mainly on the Christmas season. In reading a lot of gift related magazines, we have been exposed to the idea of having collections that change with the changing seasons. I think our inspiration for the designs seen in this collection came from those readings.

Because we didn't start off with any ideas about the set number of designs we wanted for the collection, we concentrated on themes and came up with the designs for our collection that way. Twelve would seem to be a magic number for the collection—a design for each month. In retrospect we might have done a different grouping if we had approached the idea from another angle other than twelve months, but who knows?

Weather is the determining factor for the literal change of seasons; however, seasonal designs seem to revolve more around holiday themes than the weather. To help inspire you and get you thinking of the various designs that you could come up with, I have compiled this list of seasons along with their corresponding themes. Please use the list and work out some new designs of your own. Don't forget to include other holidays and special days that are important to you, such as birthdays and anniversaries. Also you should consider days or themes that are of local or state importance such as statehood or founder's days.

Season	Month	Theme	Season	Month	Theme
Winter	December	Christmas			
		Camille's Birthday	Summer	June	School Is Out
	January	New Year			Flag Day
		Father Time			Graduation
		Baby New Year			Birds
		Jack Frost			Bees
		Old Man Winter			Butterflies
		Snowmen			Gardening
		Skaters			Weddings
		Skiers			Summer Fun Stuff
	February	Valentine's Day		July	Independence Day
		President's Day			The Sunshine
		George Washington			The Outdoors
		Abe Lincoln			Water Sports
		M.L. King		August	More of the Same
		My Birthday	Fall	September	Labor Day
Spring	March	Ides of March			School Starts
		March Hares			Harvest
		St. Patrick's Day			Crows
		Jake's Birthday			Scarecrows
	April	Easter		October	Halloween
		April Fools (jester or clown)			Leaves Changing Color
		Tax Day			Harvest
		Chicks			Full Moon
		Bunnies			Our Wedding Anniversary
	May	Flowers		November	Thanksgiving
		May Poles			Veteran's Day
		Memorial Day			

Chapter Two
Design Considerations,
Tips, and Patterns

In this chapter, we have provided 10 full-size patterns that correspond to the pieces shown in the book. You are free to use these for your own pleasure but please remember that these will be the basis for some items in my reproduction collection. Please don't use them for commercial purposes. You can easily come up with your own designs by modifying mine or creating your own from scratch.

I designed the patterns after first inspecting the various door frames in my home to get an idea of how much space is available. I measured between the top of the molding and the ceiling as well as between the edge of the side molding and the nearest wall. These designs easily fit in my own house, but you should look around your house in case there are significant differences.

The work pieces that I will be using were cut out of 1-inch basswood which actually was 1-inch thick instead of ¾ of an inch. The depth or thickness of the molding is of some concern, but there is really no need to carve the pieces down to the same thickness as the molding. You can see that many of my pieces extend beyond the molding. When you display the piece in your home over a door, you will want to secure it using some sticky putty, double-sided tape, or a similar technique.

When designing each piece, I considered whether it would rest to the right or left side of the door frame. Notice that some pieces can only sit at the left side and some only at the right side. Though, there is one piece—the one with the two snowmen—that can sit at either side. When you set off on your own to design a piece, please consider where the piece will fit best and have the most impact and plan accordingly.

WEE BIT OF GOOD LUCK

USE OUR SLOGAN OR COME UP WITH ONE OF YOUR OWN.

TRY THIS ONE "ERIN GO BRAGH"

GOLD

FULL SIZE PATTERN

CUT FROM 1" BASSWOOD

DON'T FORGET THE SHAMROCKS AND FOUR LEAF CLOVER.

SPRING BUNNY

DRESS THE BUNNY
UP — TOP HAT, COAT,
VEST, WHATEVER.

FULL SIZE PATTERN

CUT OUT OF 1" BASSWOOD

PUT A DESIGN ON
THE CARROT

©98

THANKFUL "TOM"

FULL SIZE PATTERN

CUT FROM 1" BASSWOOD

PUT YOUR OWN DESIGN ON HIS SIGN.

TRY OUR SLOGAN OR ONE OF YOUR OWN.

©99

GIMME A HAND

THIS PATTERN
CAN GO RIGHT
OR LEFT.

FULL SIZE PATTERN

CUT FROM 1" BASSWOOD

PUT YOUR OWN FACES
ON THESE FELLOWS.

ADD YOUR OWN
DECORATIONS TO
HATS, SCARVES, ETC.

©98

WHAT WOULD UNCLE SAM
HOLD INSTEAD OF A
FIRECRACKER?

FULL SIZE PATTERN

CUT FROM 1" BASSWOOD

PUT YOUR OWN DESIGN
ON THE FLAG.

FRIENDLY WITCH

HELPING
HAND

FULL SIZE PATTERN

CUT FROM 1" BASSWOOD

PUT YOU OWN DESIGN ON
THE CAT FACE AND THE
GHOSTS

ADD MORE GHOSTS.

© 98

MAN OVERBOARD

MAKE
SOMETHING
PEEK OUT OF
A WINDOW.

FULL SIZE PATTERN

CUT FROM 1" BASSWOOD

YOU CAN ADD SOME
MORE CREATURES -
MAYBE HANGING DOWN
FROM NOAH'S FEET.

© 98

THE MAN ON THE MOON

HAPPY BEAR

PUT SOMETHING
CUTE ON BEAR'S
HAT.

MAYBE A REAL
"FLY."

SIMPLE
BASKET
WEAVE

WORMS

BAIT

FULL SIZE PATTERN

CUT OUT OF I" BASSWOOD

SHALLOW "U" GOUGE
GIVES LOOK OF "SCALES"

HANG IN THERE

YOU CAN GIVE
SANTA A DIFFERENT
BAG - WITH MORE
STUFF.

FULL SIZE PATTERN

CUT FROM 1" BASSWOOD

GIVE SANTA A
DIFFERENT HAT.

COULD SOMETHING BE
HANGING FROM
HIS FEET ?

©98

Other design considerations must include how far along the top of the door and how far down the side of the door you would like the piece to extend. Different combinations will work and there doesn't seem to be any special magic involved in these decisions. It is important, however, to have the horizontal part at least twice as long as the horizontal dimension of the hanging part to counterbalance the weight of the hanging part. You can't really have a skimpy little piece on top of the molding with a big one hanging down the side.

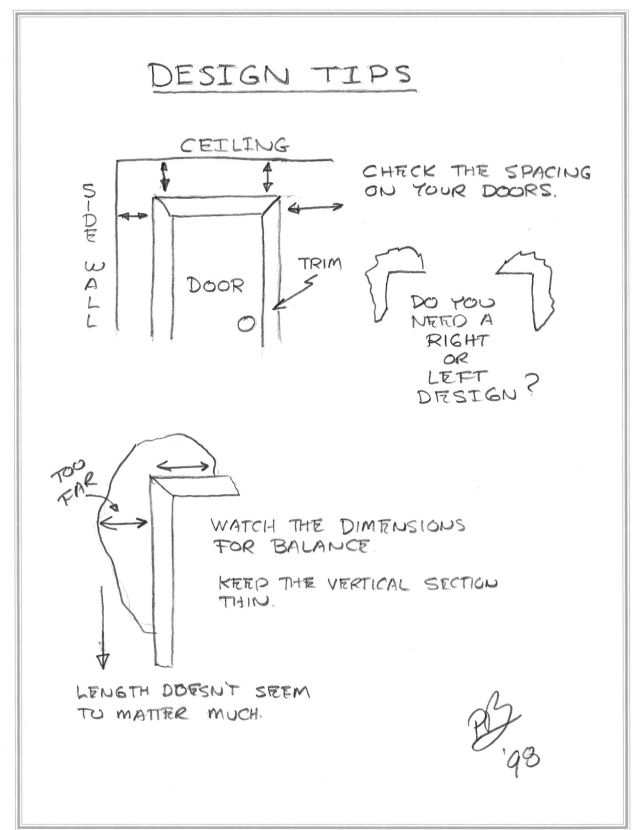

Chapter Three
Carving the Leprechaun

I used as few tools as possible to carve these pieces to keep the work simple. The designs were left open in some areas to allow Camille to paint some extras on the designs. You can carve and paint the details as you wish.

These days I don't do much relief carving, so I don't have any special hold down devices or techniques to make it easier. I suggest you try securing the work piece to a larger piece of stock by screwing through the stock into the back of the work piece. This will allow you to clamp the stock securely but will also leave enough room for you to work on the piece.

I carve quickly using hand tools until I get to a point where the work is almost finished. Then I use a Foredom rotary tool with ruby and diamond bits to clean up the piece. Each piece is sanded with a flap sander and then also sanded by hand to prepare it for painting.

When relief carving, you need to know the intended depth of each area of the pattern. Sometimes it is helpful to set in the deepest areas first to establish a maximum depth for the entire carving. However, in these pieces the maximum depth occurs at the edges so it is not necessarily helpful to carve these sections first. Here, I have included some tips on relief carving to help you.

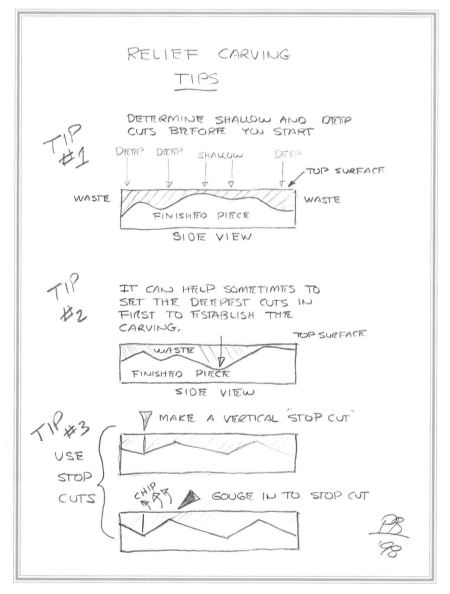

Almost every cut to remove wood is preceded by a "stop cut." This is a vertical cut made down into the piece to provide a place where the angled cut will naturally stop and where the forming chip of wood can release. Stop cuts are made with a knife, a straight gouge, or a shaped gouge depending on the line to be followed.

You need to be careful while carving these pieces because the point where the horizontal section joins the vertical or hanging section is particularly weak due to the grain in the wood.

Closely look over the finished Leprechaun before you start to work. You need to think in terms of the highest and lowest points on the carving in order to get an idea in your mind of the contours needed for each piece. Notice on this piece that the two banners are the farthest down and that the vertical centerline is the highest. See how the pot of gold is shaped and how the gold pieces stick up out of the pot. You can see that his fingers must be behind the banners because you can see only his thumbs in the front. Check out his pants and stockings as well as his shoes. Familiarize yourself with these details so you can re-create them in your carving.

This is the finished Leprechaun. Look the piece over carefully before starting your own carving. Visualize the different depths of the carving as if you were looking down on it from above.

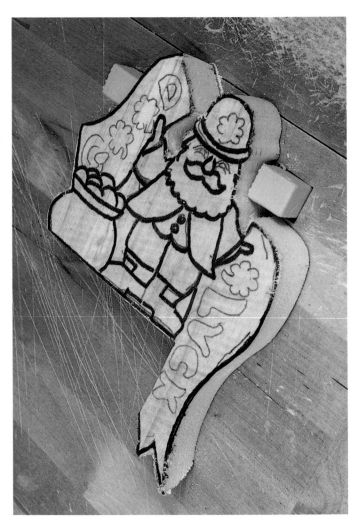

This is the Leprechaun (Good Luck) piece on my work bench before I started carving. The piece was sawed from a 1-inch section of basswood after I transferred the pattern using carbon paper. I don't do much flat carving so I don't have a great hold-down system. Brute force works for me. The two blue-gray blocks on either side of the work piece are bench "dogs" or stops.

This side view shows the relative thickness of the work piece compared to the door frame and molding in my house. You can see that the work piece is quite a bit thicker than the trim, but, of course, we will carve a good bit of that away.

I used as few tools as possible for this project partly so you could follow along and partly so the bench top wouldn't be so cluttered. Here I started carving with a shallow "U" gouge to outline a corner of the beard. This relief carving will consist mainly of outlining an area with a stop cut and then removing the waste wood as needed.

In relief carving an important first step is to identify mentally the areas of the carving that will be the "highest" and the sections that will be the "lowest." As you look at the Leprechaun and think about his pose, you know that there will be a vertical center line that will be the highest and he will fade off to the left and right. His beard, nose, front hat brim, shoe tips, and pot of gold will be the "highest."

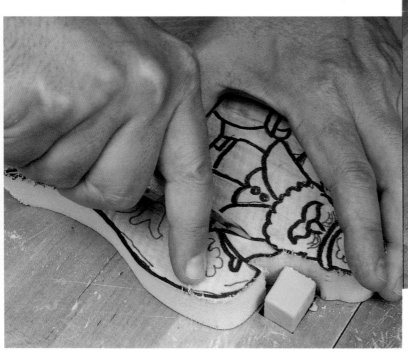

Outline the arm using a knife.

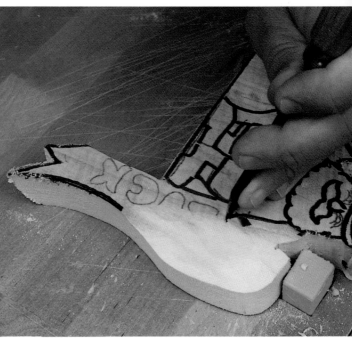

Use a medium "U" gouge to stop cut below the coat.

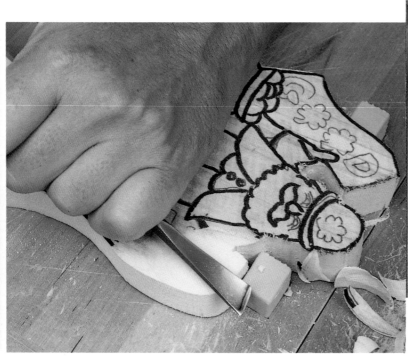

Remove the wood outside of the stop cut on the arm. This area will taper off to the right. I used a wide shallow "U" gouge to remove the wood.

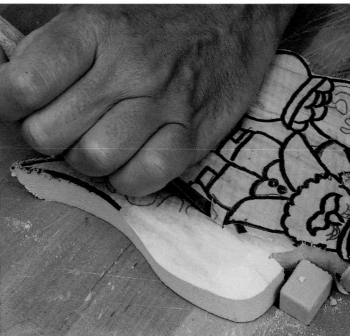

Remove waste wood below the cut.

Push the waste area lower by removing another layer of waste wood.

Here I turned the piece around against the bench dogs (stops) to taper the lower end of the banner down.

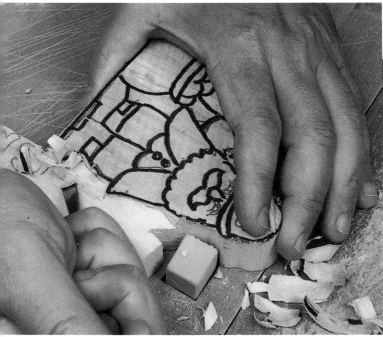

Note how I changed grip here to get rid of some of the wood under my hand. With a more secure hold on the piece you can continue to work in a more straightforward manner.

Taper the banner down as you wish. The lower end of the banner will be one of the thinnest areas of the finished carving. It will actually be thinner than the door trim.

Cut the outline deeper with a knife.

Use a "U" gouge to outline the bottom of the coat.

Remove more wood outside the cut.

Remove the wood below the cut.

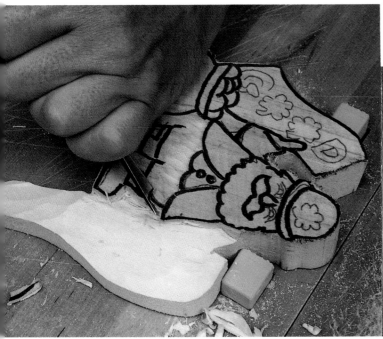

Remember that the pants will not be flat; they will "bump up" where the knees should be. So think about it before you remove too much wood.

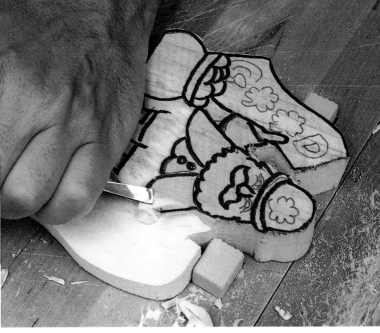

Remove some of the wood from the coat, tapering towards the bottom of the beard.

Cut a stop cut at the bottom of the beard.

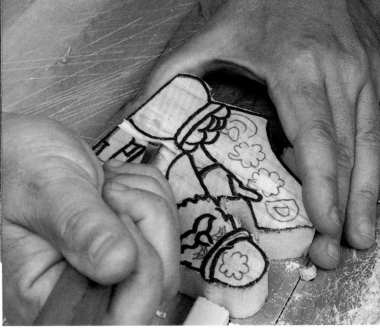

Put a stop cut along the side of the pot of gold. Then remove some of the pants and shoes to define the separation.

Make a stop cut to separate the bottom of the pot of gold from the top.

Here is where we stand right now. We will go back over some of these same areas again later since carving is a process similar to "peeling an onion." By that I mean we peel away small layers at a time in order to reveal the finished product. Taking too much off at one time can throw the piece off balance. Take it slow and easy.

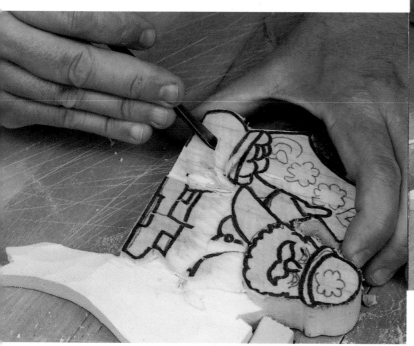

Remove the wood from the lower part of the pot, tapering down into the stop cut. You will want a rounded pot so make sure you think about the shape before you remove too much wood.

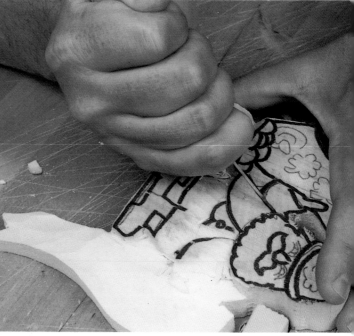

Make a stop cut along the arm and coat on the left side.

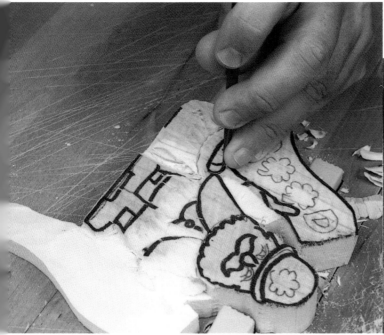

Remove some wood from the arm area. Make stop cuts along the lines as needed to keep the different areas defined.

Remove the waste wood from the banner. Taper the banner down as far as you wish. Note that you will lose the definition of the hand here but you can redraw it later. Also note that I am not going to carve the slogan onto the ribbon. Camille will paint that on freestyle. Even if you are going to carve the slogan, you will still want to trim the banner down and redraw your design.

Remove the wood from above the gold pieces that will stick up from the pot of gold.

Taper the banner and arm, making it drop down toward the left side. Get the left side as thin as you wish but certainly not as thin as the right side which you have already tapered.

Here is where we are right now.

Remove some of the vest inside the coat. Don't take too much. Remember that the centerline of the figure will be the highest part when the carving is done.

Outline the inner edges of the coat.

Before starting to work on any new areas, I will go back over some of the ones we have done to remove some more wood and make the definition of these areas clearer.

More clean-up.

Shape the coat more, leaving it high in the center and tapered at the edges.

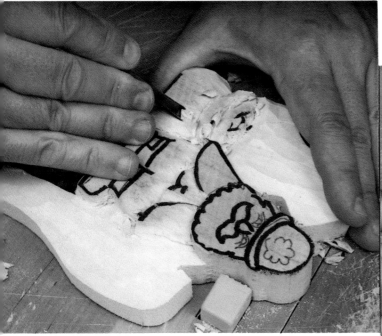

More clean-up.

More coat work.

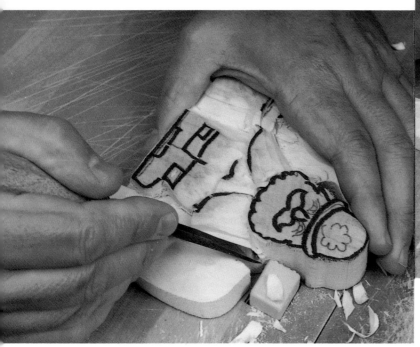

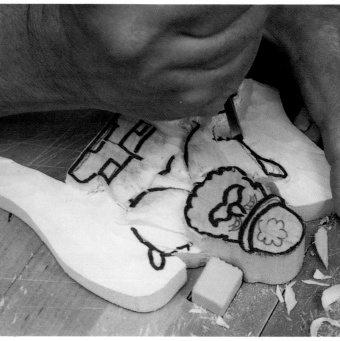

Outline the sleeves and thumb area.

Taper the figure down around the side of the head.

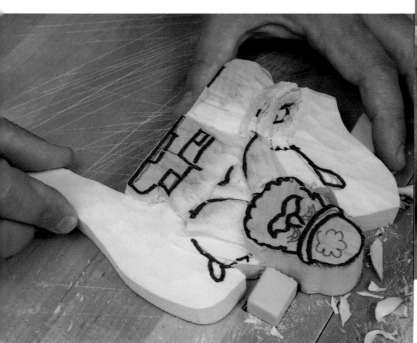

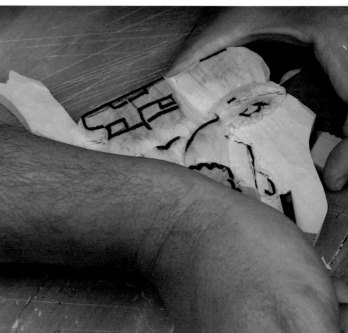

Remove banner wood from outside the sleeve and thumb. Cut a line separating the sleeve from the thumb and define the thumb a little.

Here is where we are right now. Note that I have redrawn the arms and thumbs back onto the work piece. I referred to the pattern and drew the lines freehand onto the piece.

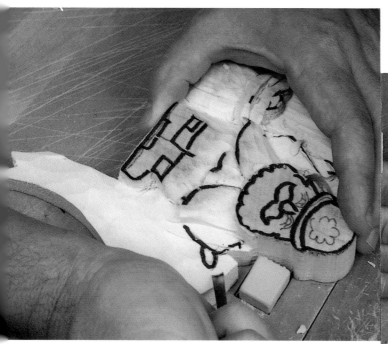

Do the same to the other side.

Remove wood from outside of the figure to highlight it.

Define the thumb too.

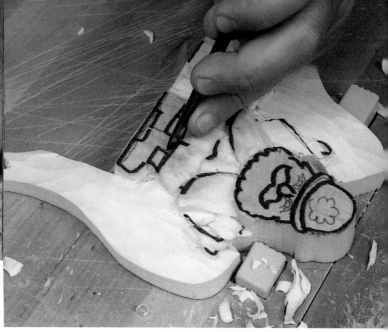

Outline the shoes.

31

Outline both sides.

Shape the shoes starting at the toes and moving toward the heels. The toes will be the highest with the heel cut deeper into the piece. There will actually be some stockings or leggings showing above the shoes and below the pantaloons when we are done. During this process you will cut away the definition lines for the shoe buckles. Don't worry, you can redraw them later.

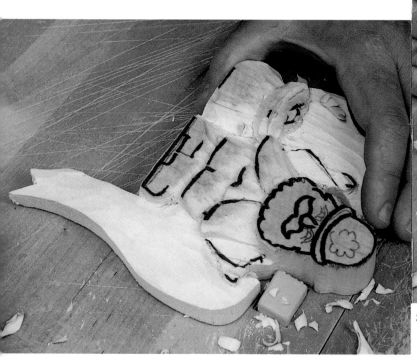

Here is where we are at this point. We have pretty much defined the figure and the pot of gold. We still have more defining and shaping to do before we get to the face.

Shape the shoes and stocking areas.

32

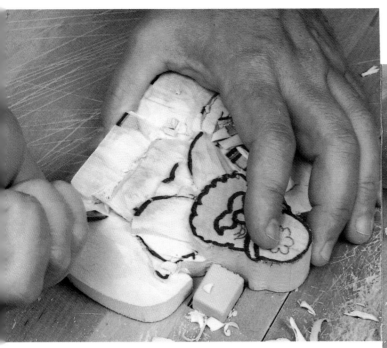

You may have to cut the outline deeper as you shape the shoe to keep a good separation from the wood outside the shoe.

Cut a deep line between the two heels.

Shape the pants as you go.

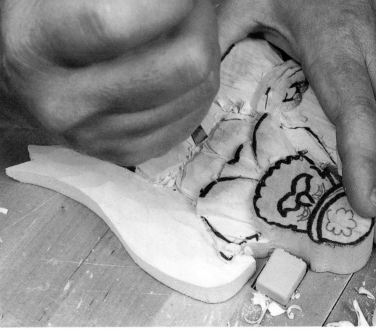

Deepen the definition between the pantaloons.

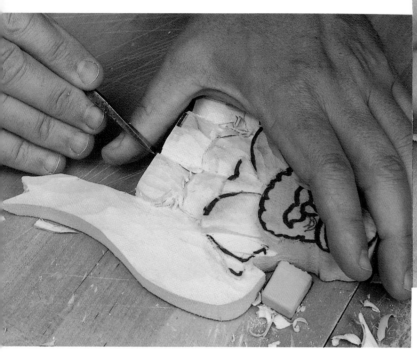

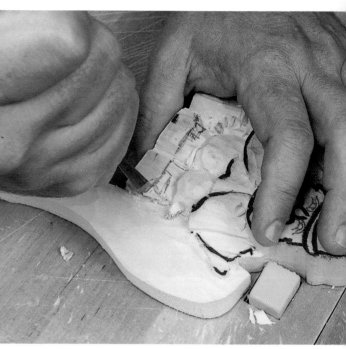

Cut away from the outside of the buckles. The area above the buckles and below the pantaloons will be the stockings.

Taper the heels of the shoes down toward the cut.

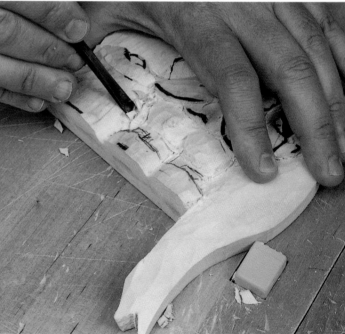

Define the shoes and buckles. You may have to carve additional wood away from the outside of the shoes to better define them.

Redraw the shoe tops and shoe buckles. Refer to the pattern if you need to.

Cut a clear definition along the tops of the shoes.

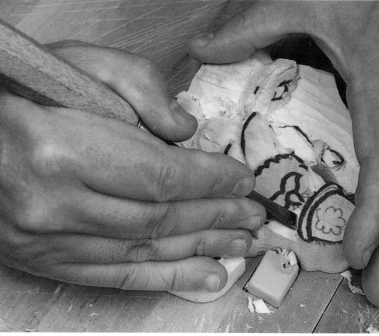

On the head, first outline the bottom of the hat brim and then remove wood from the forehead up to the brim.

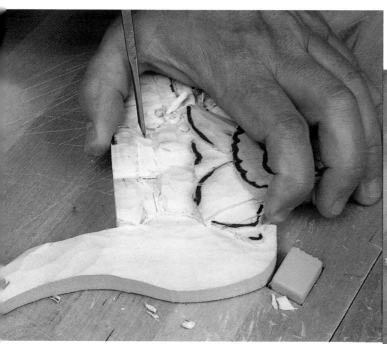

Remove the stocking wood above the shoes and below the pantaloons.

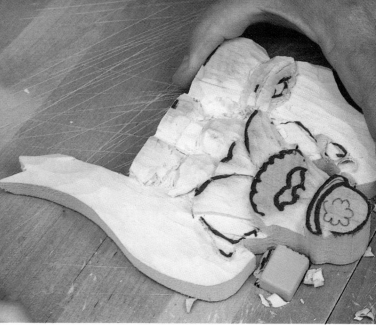

Shape the sides of the head. Remember: the centerline will be the highest, so taper out and down.

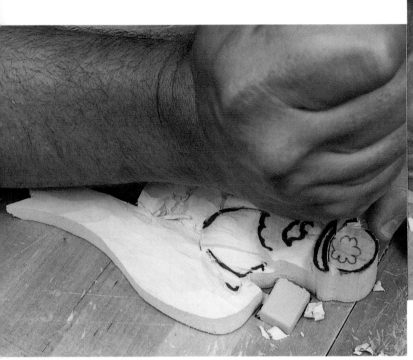

Outline the top of the hat brim.

Shape the hat like a bowler hat. I turned the piece back around so you could get a good look at it.

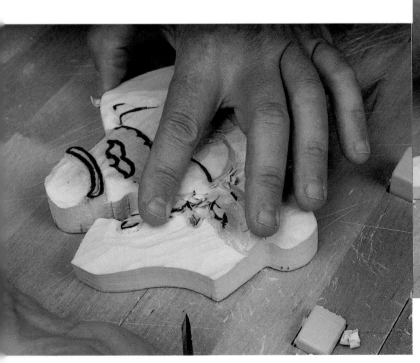

Round off the top of the bowler hat. I turned the piece upside down to get a better angle for carving.

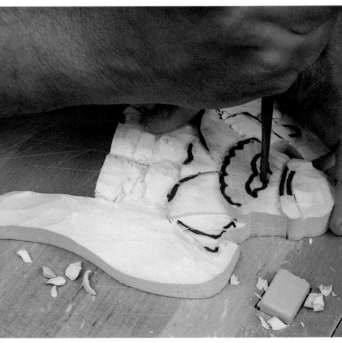

Outline the bottom of the nose. I used a small "U" gouge to cut a semi-circle under the nose.

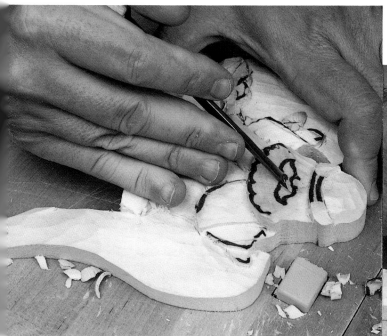

Run up to the stop cut under the nose by removing wood from the mustache area.

Outline the bottom of the mustache using a "U" gouge.

To help define the nose, cut away more of the forehead area and more wood from the sides of the nose.

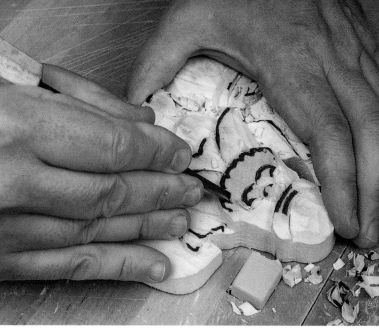

Run up to the stop cut under the mustache to remove wood from the beard and define the mustache.

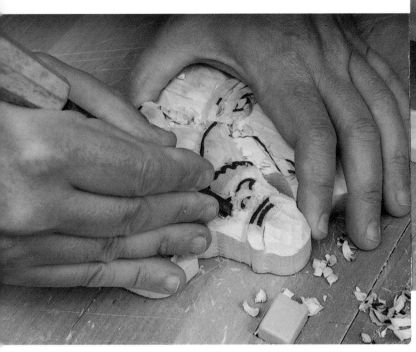

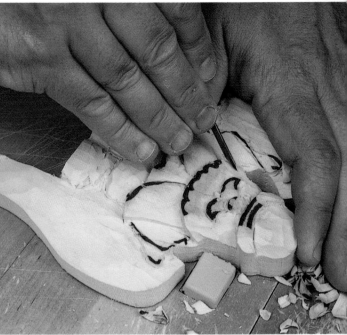

Round off the sides of the beard.

Shape the mustache a little. There isn't much wood to work with so be careful.

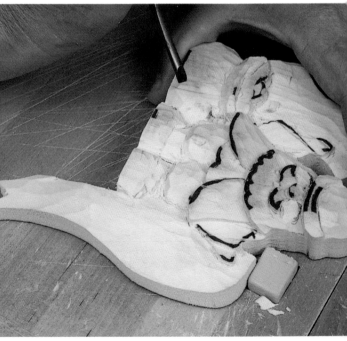

Redraw the lines for the eyes.

Here is what the piece looks like at this stage. The face is fairly well defined but needs some more work before it will be complete.

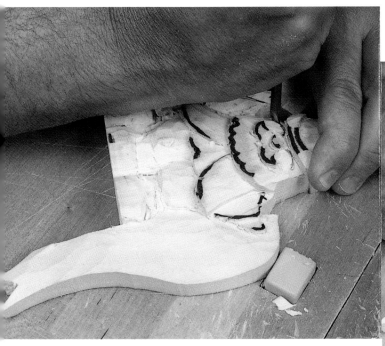

Use a small "U" gouge in an inverted position to cut the eye area along the lines. I drew the lines so they would fit the small gouge I intended to use. You could use a knife too if you are careful.

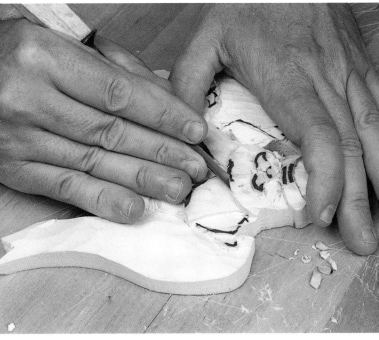

Shape the beard more making it a smooth curve from the center out to both sides.

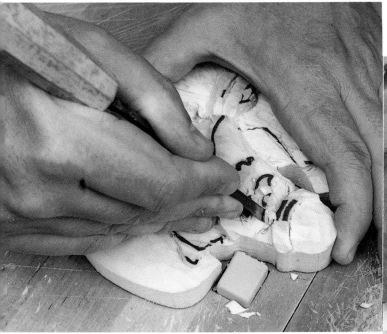

Clean the wood out from the eye socket. I make the eye sockets on these figures very simple: really nothing more than a rounded area under the brow where Camille can paint the eye.

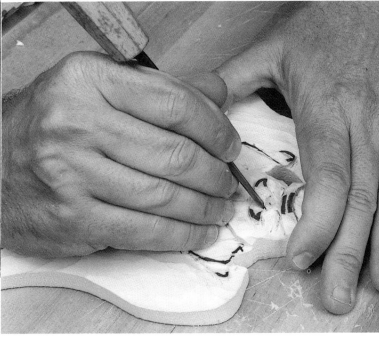

Outline the top of the mustache and clean out a little wood from above the mustache. This will highlight the mustache and also make the cheeks more defined.

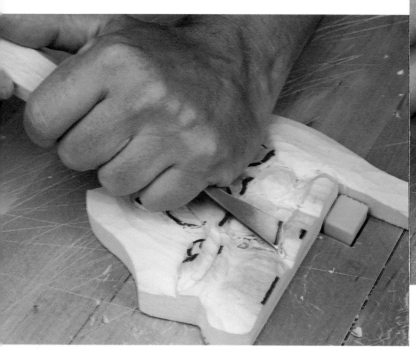

Taper away the bottom of the pot, so it is at least the thickness of the door trim.

At this point you have carved over the entire piece at least once. Now look at the piece and see where it needs more definition. In this shot I have turned the piece around and I'm working on the lower area with a larger "U" gouge.

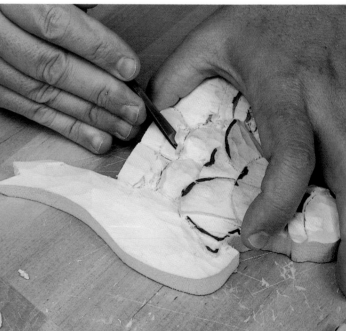

Here I am deepening the stocking area.

To make the pot of gold fuller and give it more roundness, round down the bottom of it.

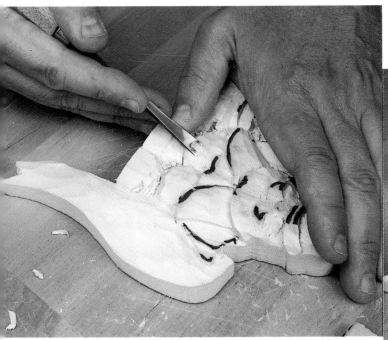

Here I am rounding the pants more.

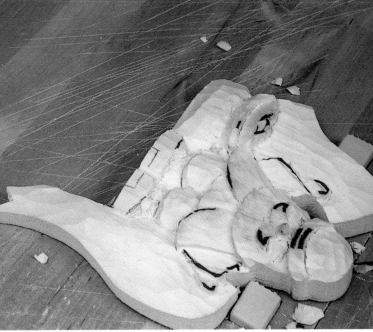

After a little more work on the vest this is what the piece looks like at this point.

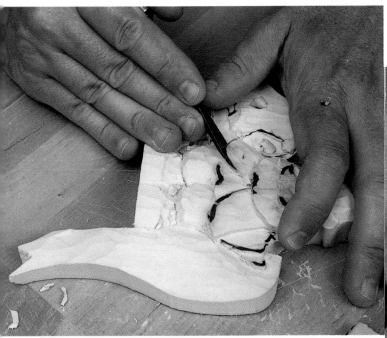

Here I am working on rounding down the coat some more.

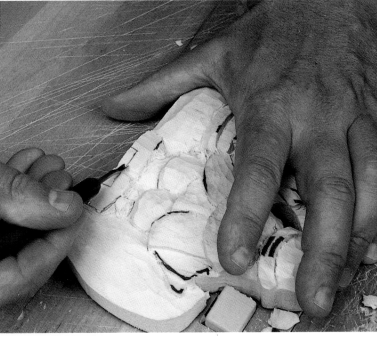

I used a small "V" gouge to outline deeply the heels of the shoes.

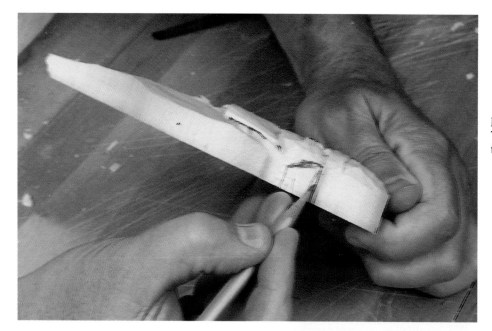

Mark a hair line on the side of the head. This will also complete the definition of the bottom of the hat.

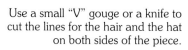

Use a small "V" gouge or a knife to cut the lines for the hair and the hat on both sides of the piece.

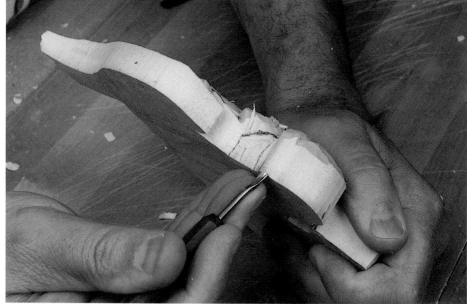

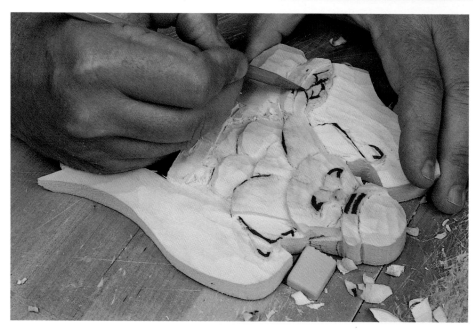

Draw in lines to define the pieces of gold in the leprechaun's pot.

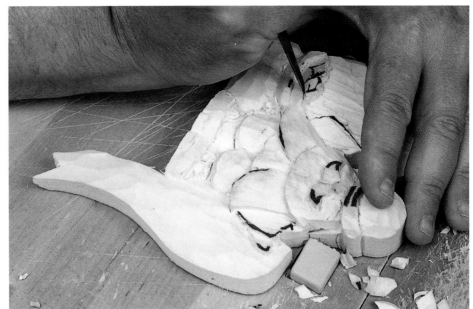

Use a small "U" gouge to define the cuts outlining the various pieces of gold.

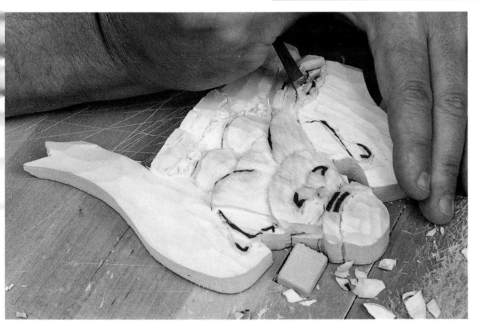

Remove small chips from above each cut to make the gold pieces look as if they are coming up out of the pot.

After taking more wood off both of the banners, I compared the thickness of the piece to the thickness of the wood trim from the door. It is a little difficult to see in this shot, but the banner thickness is the same as or less than the door trim, while the pot of gold and the shoes are slightly thicker than the trim. If you wish, you can continue to thin these areas down to match the trim. I left them as they are shown.

Chapter Four
Carving the Thankful Turkey

I used the same tools and techniques for carving the turkey as I did for the Leprechaun. Again, I didn't carve the details on the banners, but instead left these parts for Camille.

Look over the finished carving and notice the details. Which areas are the highest? Which areas are the lowest? How are the feet placed? What is the taper on the banners? How do the feathers taper?

Once you have figured out the answers to these questions, you will have in mind the contours of the piece. Now you can go ahead and give it a try.

This is the finished and painted turkey. Before you start your own carving, look over closely the various depths and details of the piece, trying to commit them to memory.

Here is the thankful turkey shown with the pattern transferred to the wood cut out. I will not carve the corn decorations onto the turkey's sign; they will be painted.

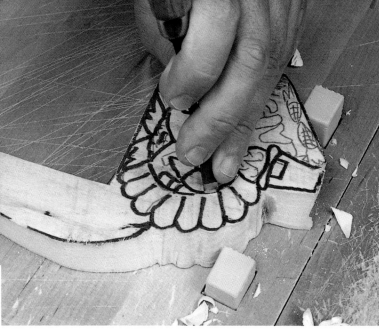

First, start by outlining the turkey's body. Think about the relief carving needed to define the high areas and the low areas. The turkey's body will be out in front on this piece.

This shot shows the thickness of the original piece compared to the door trim. The piece is about twice as thick.

Then, outline the hat.

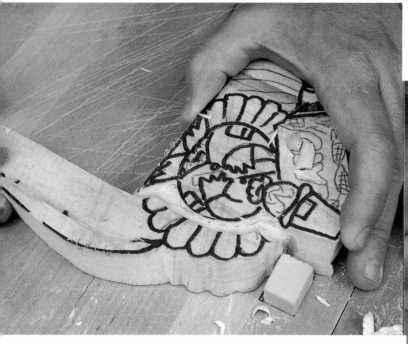

Remove wood from outside of the body. You will eliminate the pattern lines but they will be redrawn later.

Remove the feather wood area tapering it down to the outside to give the turkey some visual depth.

Remove the wood from the banner. I turned it upside down to get a good shot at it with my large shallow "U" gouge.

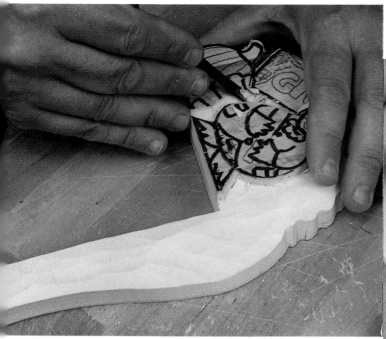

Outline the other side of the body and remove some wood from the feather area.

Carve the pumpkin down to the left to give it roundness.

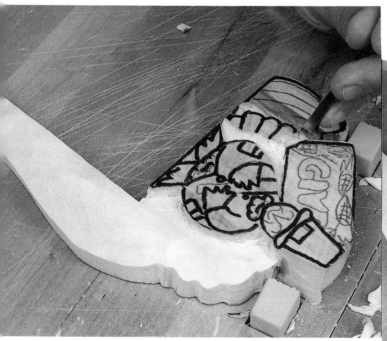

Outline the line separating the feathers from the pumpkin.

Round the top of the pumpkin too.

Outline the chin area of the turkey. Below the chin is a wattle but we'll get to that in a minute.

Shape the feathers down and out to the side.

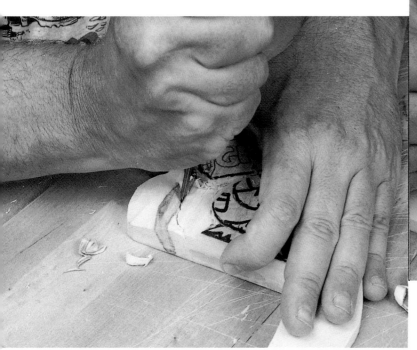

Carve away some wood to define the chin area. The wattle is carved away at this time but we will redraw the lines for it later.

Keep the definition between the pumpkin and the outer feathers.

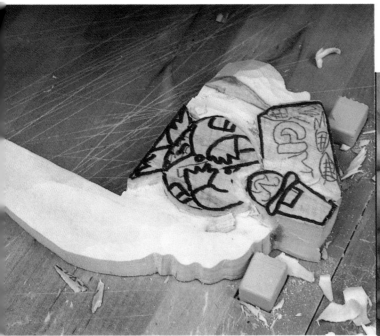

Here is where we are at this point. Note that I have done some work on the left side of the turkey's hat by carving away some of the sign.

Remove some of the feet area. Also outline the bottom of the coat to separate the belly from the coat. Remove some of the belly area.

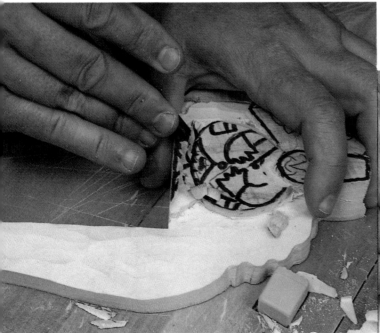

Carve a stop cut to define the tops of the feet.

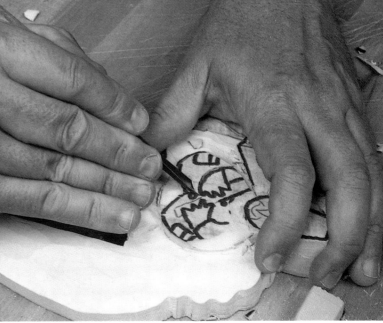

Outline the arm areas with stop cuts.

Remove some wood from the coat area outside the arms.

Outline the handle of the turkey's sign with a knife.

Carve the top of the sign down. Taper it as far back as you wish.

Outline the turkey's fingers with a small gouge or knife.

Outline the fingers of the other hand.

Make a deep cut between the turkey's feet (heels?).

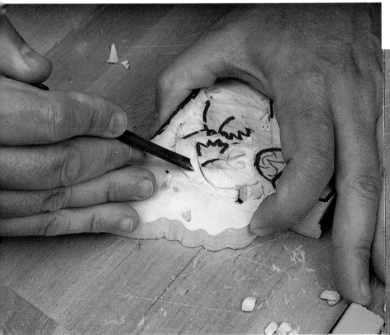

Remove more wood from outside the arms to define them further.

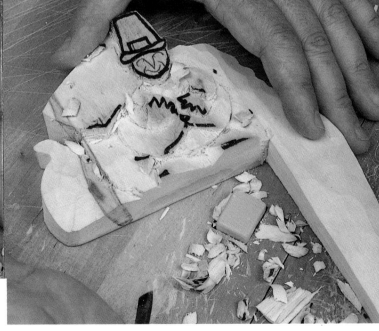

To shape the feet, carve out the wood moving toward the deep cut between the turkey's heels. Imagine that the heels are together and far back.

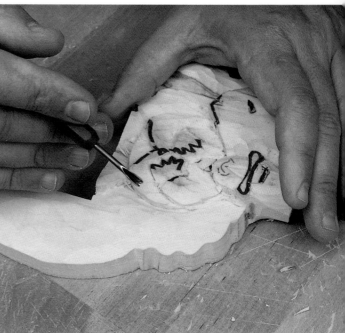

Outline the beak using a knife or a small "V" gouge as I have done.

Outline the brim of the turkey's pilgrim hat. Notice that I have started shaping the hat from above the buckle up to the top.

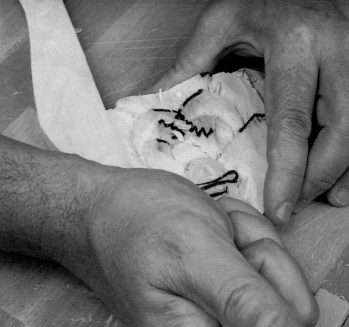

Shape the chin of the turkey down toward the wattle.

Remove some wood from below the brim of the hat. Start to shape the face back to the sides.

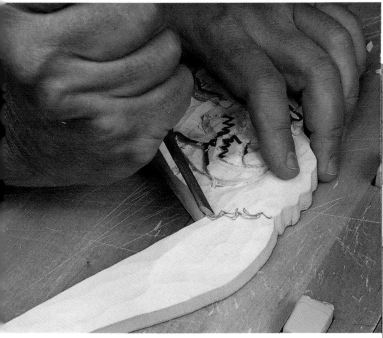

Redraw the feathers at the side to separate the banner from the turkey's body. Outline the feathers with a gouge or knife.

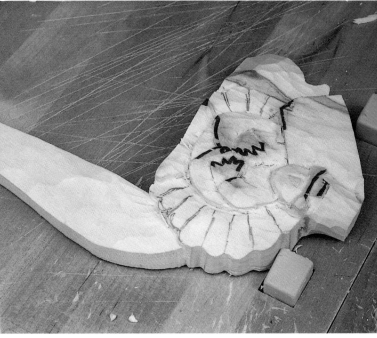

Draw the lines to distinguish the turkey's feathers. These lines radiate out from the body to the feather tips.

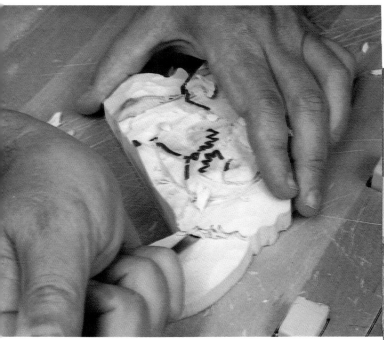

Remove some of the banner wood that lies on the outer part of the feathers.

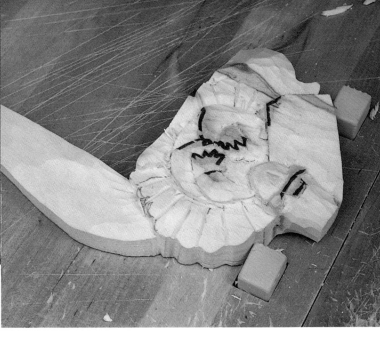

Use a knife or gouge to cut grooves along the feather edges.

Look over your piece for areas that need to be cleaned up, deepened, or highlighted more.

Deepen the lines with a gouge or knife.

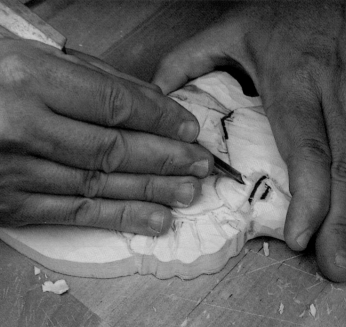

Do some clean up and touch up of these areas.

Round each feather using a gouge.

More trimming.

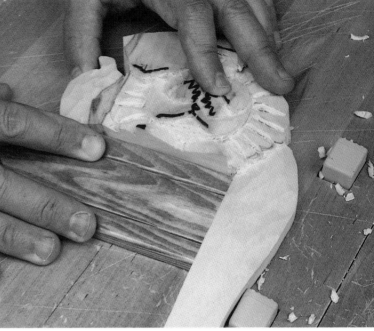

Here I am comparing the thickness of the piece to the thickness of the door trim on which it will rest. It is still too thick at this point so I must trim it down more. Remember peeling an onion goes layer by layer.

More clean up and touch up.

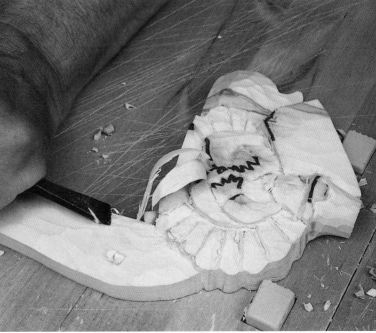

Trim down the banner.

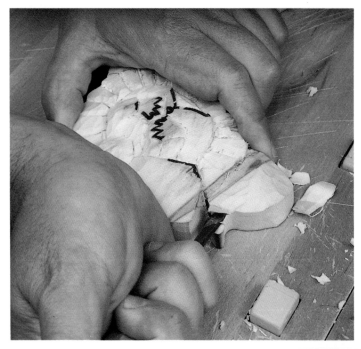

Trim down the bottom of the pumpkin.

Carve some grooves into the pumpkin. Make sure to go all the way around the left side too.

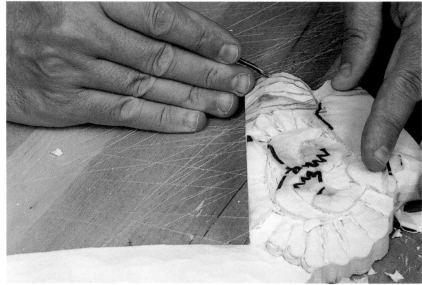

Now the thickness looks better. Notice that I didn't take any more wood off the feet, but I easily could have without causing a problem.

Note: At this point, I stop carving and grind the piece with a Foredom rotary tool using diamond bits. This cleans out the crevices and can provide some of the final details. On the turkey feathers, for example, I ground small grooves at the top edge of each feather to add some detail. You can do this with a knife or gouge too.

From this point on, I will sand the piece by hand using 400 grit paper to get a smooth finish for painting.

Chapter Five
Painting the Leprechaun

You can pretty much choose any colors you want when painting the various pieces, even the Leprechaun. However, the Leprechaun is a very specific image of Ireland and probably should remain close to the traditional colors. For instance, you could do a green hat, green coat, and green shoes. You may want to combine light against dark green on these pieces to help define the carved areas. Paul didn't carve many of the details on this piece leaving the job of decorating the piece to me.

As usual, the piece was given a base coat of White Lightning stain and sealer by J.W. Etc. This provides a smooth white surface for painting.

You don't need to do all the details the way they are shown here. Think about the subject matter and decide what little extras would make it more appealing. Shamrocks and four leaf clovers are a natural for Irish themes.

For this project, Delta Ceramcoat acrylic paints were used. The exact colors used were:

Fleshtone
Butter Yellow
Spice Brown
Black
GLEAMS 14K Gold
Hunter Green
White
Napthol Red Light
Copen Blue

This is the piece after it has been sanded and the White Lightning has been applied.

Hunter Green was used for the jacket.

The face and hands are painted with Fleshtone.

Paint the hat, pants, and shoes black.

The banners are painted with Butter Yellow. Later on I wondered about this color selection being so close to the gold pieces. An optional color for the banners would be tan or a light blue.

Paint the gold pot Spice Brown.

Float a little Naptha Red over the Fleshtone on the face.

Paint the gold pieces with GLEAMS 14K Gold. Also paint the shoe buckles gold.

To paint the eyes follow these steps: put down a base layer of White and let it dry, Copen Blue goes over the White for the iris, a smaller Black dot in the middle, and then a small White dot for a highlight on the iris. I also lined the eyes with Spice Brown which had been slightly watered down.

59

To get the details onto the piece follow these steps: add a line down the center of the vest, put some buttons on the vest using the rounded end of the brush, line the socks with Hunter Green which has been slightly thinned, put white stitches on the coat, and dip the fat end of a bigger brush into the Gold paint to make neat gold buttons on the coat. I put a four leaf clover on the hat in green outlined with white.

At this point the paint on the figure needs to be sealed. I use Grumbacher Final Fixative Matte finish spray.
I outlined the lettering on the banners with a black Sharpie pen. Inside the lettering I added Hunter Green. The Shamrocks on the banners add a cute touch. Be careful to avoid a heavy spray of fixative over the Sharpie since it can cause the Sharpie ink to run.

Here is the Spring Bunny. This is a simple piece to carve with few details, but it still catches the eye. You can do many variations on the bunny and carrot theme.

These two snowmen are helping each other. This piece can be turned either left or right making it more versatile. The white gloves probably would be better as a different color since they tend to fade out against a white wall.

This is the painted Thankful Turkey that I carved in Chapter Four. Note the extra carved details on the feathers and all the painted decorations that Camille added.

Here the snowmen are turned the other direction.

The Friendly Witch is giving a hand to the three little ghosts hanging down the edge. The pumpkin, black cat, broom, and tombstone in the back finish up the theme. The ghosts fade some against a white wall. To help, light gray could be used for highlighting on their sides.

It's a Grand Old Flag shows Uncle Sam holding a firecracker. Stars, flags, stripes and the red, white, and blue colors make this piece very patriotic.

Man Overboard! Noah is getting a helping "hand" from his elephant buddy as he hangs down the side of the door. A Noah theme can be great fun since you can select your own animals. I used sheep, a giraffe, a cat, a bird, and the helpful elephant.

This bear has caught his greatest dream – a fish so big he is struggling to get it landed. You can do different fish and different bear themes for your works. The bear possibilities are limitless.

The man on the moon is Santa and he is hanging high. I particularly like the moon face in this piece. A moon theme would be good all by itself, if you can work out the details of, say, a harvest moon.

Santa is hanging onto his bag and scrambling for a toe hold. I'm sure it all works out in the end. The bag, the toys, even the Santa can be different in your piece.

Here is something you don't want to find on your doorstep – me! This is one of the woodcarver T-shirts my brother Bruce designs. Maybe you've seen them in *Chip Chats* magazine. If you want to know how to get a T-shirt drop me a line at 4405 S. Echo Ct., Spokane, Wa. 99223.